All Movies Love the Moon

ADVANCE PRAISE FOR
ALL MOVIES LOVE THE MOON

"Gregory Robinson's *All Movies Love the Moon* brings silent film, that drowned and nearly forgotten continent, back to life and into our time. From the hand-colored fantasy of Méliès' *A Trip to the Moon* to Hitchcock's chilling thriller *The Lodger*, each of these prose poems is a movie—one filled with the sheer joy we take in watching as the projector's light illuminates the darkness."
—**JESSE LEE KERCHEVAL**, author of *Cinema Muto* and *My Life as a Silent Movie*

"In the eighteenth century Laurence Sterne broke all the rules of novel-writing that hadn't yet been written with *Tristram Shandy*. In 2013 Gregory Robinson's *All Movies Love the Moon* travels back in time to the dawn of cinema, when silent movies were as surreal, playful, dislocating, and dumbfounding as the twentieth century itself. In deadpan prose poems Robinson tracks the gradual emergence of narrative out of the dream logic of pure images, and the more sudden birth of pop culture as we know it, until we see Theda Bara and Sylvester Stallone silently side by side at last. The poetry in film, the film in poetry: the book is a delirious romp through the grammar of their entanglement."
—**JOSHUA COREY**, author of *Beautiful Soul: An American Elegy*

"*All Movies Love the Moon* is as much the autobiography of a cinéaste as a history of silent film and the linguistic windows through which it makes meaning. Interspersed with real and invented intertitles to guide us through his poetic underworld, Gregory Robinson's prose poems conduct a cinematic séance in which an array of personal and celluloid spirits parade before the reader. Inquiry gives way to elegy both historical and personal, and the book's great trick is 'to bend trust without breaking it, to lead by the hand rather than by the wrist' as Robinson guides us gradually into the imaginative space between words on a screen."
—**AMARANTH BORSUK**, author of *Handiwork*

All Movies Love the Moon

Prose Poems on Silent Film

By GREGORY ROBINSON

Rose Metal Press

2014

Rose Metal Press, Inc.
P.O. Box 1956
Brookline, MA 02446
rosemetalpress@gmail.com
www.rosemetalpress.com

Library of Congress Control Number: 2014930147

ISBN: 978-0-9887645-5-2

Front cover art and design by Lillian Ling
Book design by Heather Butterfield

This book is manufactured in the United States of America and printed on acid-free paper.

To Joan Paulette, my silent film star

ACKNOWLEDGMENTS

Thank you to the editors of the following publications in which these poems first appeared, sometimes in slightly different versions:

Floodplane: "Intolerance (1916)," "He Who Gets Slapped (1924)," and "Tillie the Toiler (1927)"
Lux: "How It Feels To Be Run Over (1900)"
Magic Lantern Review: "The European Rest Cure (1904)" and "The Birth of a Nation (1915)"

I am so very grateful to:

Abigail Beckel and Kathleen Rooney for all their work on this book;
Adam Davis, Audrey Balzart, and Ed Fuentes for creating the book trailer;
Vicki and Steve Robinson for taking me to the movies;
Ed Lover and John Hazard, my best friends;
Gwen Sharp, Robin Cresiski, and Erika Beck for far more than I can ever list;

Joanna Shearer, Leila Pazargadi, Pete La Chapelle, Shirli Brautbar, Elizabeth De La Torre, Andy Kuniyuki, Tony Scinta, Rich Yao, Chris Harris, Ed Price, Kate Hahn, Ernesto Hernandez, Jr., Angela Brommel, Jonathan Dunning, Lance Hignite, Wendi Benson, Melissa Dengler, Laura Naumann, and Shantal Marshall for making my ordinary days completely extraordinary.

TABLE OF CONTENTS

PART III: THE END OF SILENTS

INTRODUCTION

In 1894, Fred Ott sneezed. Thomas Edison's cameras were there to transform the event into a motion picture, appropriately named *Record of a Sneeze*. Edison immediately copyrighted the movie to be sure no one else filmed someone sneezing without paying him royalties. The five-second action film that played for one person looking through a peephole into a giant box wasn't exactly *The Matrix*, but Edison knew he had a good thing going and he was not about to share it.

And yet moving images proved hard to contain. They chafed at confines and one-man audiences. A year or so after Ott's sneeze, two French inventors named Auguste and Louis Lumière made a machine that could record, develop, and project moving images onto a screen: the *Cinématographe Lumière*. In 1895, the first movie they exhibited to an audience showed a crowd of men, women, horses, and dogs leaving a factory. They called it *Workers Leaving the Lumière Factory*, just in case anyone was unclear. The Lumière Brothers marketed the movie as a technical achievement, a way of showing off their contraption, but the images had another idea entirely: the doors had opened and multitudes poured forth. It would be a long time getting them all back inside, into the confines of genre, convention, and profitability.

This wild escapism is what I love about silent movies. They are images that broke free, first from stillness and then from their creators. For the 30 years that followed *Workers Leaving the Factory*, the movie industry would busy itself corralling movies again, cramming stories into genres, developing patents and intellectual property. But before silent movies could be tamed, they were impulsive and unpredictable, and it is no surprise that these loosely connected images often left early audiences confused. It was hard to tell who was who and why that man was hitting the other with a shovel.

Initially, theaters hired orators to stand next to the movie and speak, imitating the voices and narrating the story for the viewers. This method eventually proved impractical, and so the use of filmed text in the form of title cards became more common. In the very early days, title cards were used to introduce sections of the movie, like chapter titles in books. As movies grew both in length and complexity, the cards took on new roles, such as representing speech, conveying the passage of time, and revealing characters' hidden thoughts. When talking films arrived, title cards disappeared within a few years, but audible voices never replaced the text's functionality. For example, in *His Picture in the Papers* (1916), a woman kisses Douglas Fairbanks after kissing a rather dull vegetarian. The title card reads:

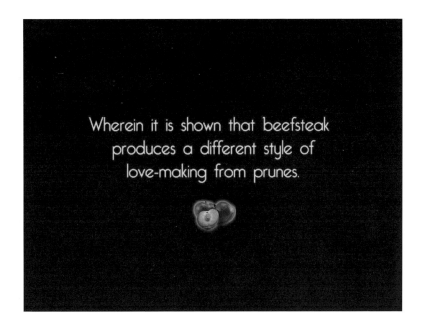

Wherein it is shown that beefsteak
produces a different style of
love-making from prunes.

So true. A character is not saying or thinking this, and it does nothing to advance the plot. Rather, it is the voice of the movie speaking directly to you, commenting alongside you, jeering its own characters. Title cards were silent film's Statler and Waldorf.

By the late 1920s, every studio had writers on staff who specialized in this kind of cinematic haiku. Ralph Spence, one of the highest paid title card writers of the time, advertised himself as a film doctor, a writer who could take unfunny films and make them watchable again just by changing the text. He was a cinematic recycler. His tagline was "All bad little movies when they die go to Ralph Spence."

There were many bad little movies, but Spence knew that the right text at the right time could turn a gallimaufry of images into a comprehensible chain of events. *All Movies Love the Moon* makes a similar attempt, connecting disparate pieces of silent movie history and finding in those intersections points of egress, single frames that expand rhizomatically once cut from the reel.

There is real history here as well, verifiable names and dates. However, if you really want to know the truth about silent movies and the words they contain, this book will provide little assistance. Then again, neither will *Title Cards and Silent Cinema* by Robert F. Samson, *Reading Silent Movies* by Linda Ireland, or *Intertitles: Some Assistance* by Stephen E. Dunn. The benefit of this book is that it will not teach you about the topic in a fraction of the time it takes to read the others, and it will do so with much better pictures.

All Movies Love the Moon

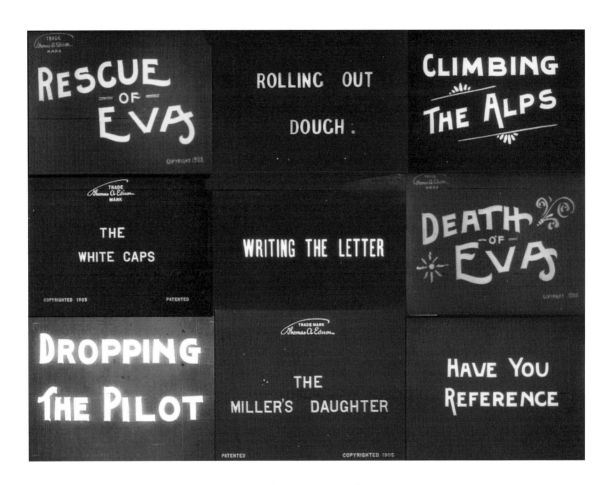

FIGURE 1: In the cinema of attractions, movies often spoke in three-word bursts.

PART I: THE CINEMA OF ATTRACTIONS

In film journals, movies made from 1893 to 1908 are commonly labeled the "cinema of attractions." Unlike the feature length films of the 1910s and 1920s, these short movies openly acknowledged the viewer, breaking the fourth wall at will. They often assumed that viewers already knew the story they were telling. The thrill was not the tale itself, but watching it come alive.

It was 1910 when Ralph Spence fell in love with movies, or so he tells me. It is hard to know when he is lying, and he drinks a lot, so he lies a lot. The ability to prevaricate effortlessly and imbibe incessantly helped him meet all the right people in Hollywood—helped him become a famous-then-forgotten writer. He stops by in dreams sometimes, always in a suit, hair slicked back and a Martini in hand. He does not seem to care that the look has gone out of style or that I might be busy. We make jokes about silent pictures, and he name drops constantly—*so I said to Fairbanks, you need to do a pirate movie*. Annoying. When I can get him sidetracked, he talks about the movies he collected, how his first wife set his collection on fire while he was asleep in the house.

He stops, sips his drink, and I let him change the topic—a well-worn story about going to Hollywood to become a screenwriter and finding a niche in writing the text for title cards. *You would not believe what they paid me*, he says, *just for a few words*. He is right. I do not believe him. But I worry if I don't listen to him, no one will.

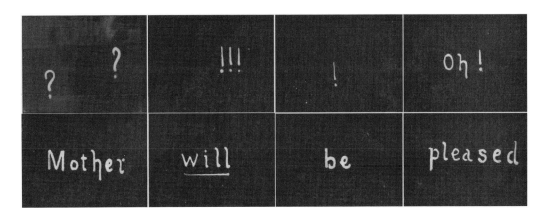

FIGURE 2: Cinema's enigmatic first words were scraped directly into the celluloid, as if it were skin. They appear the instant a car crashes into the audience.

HOW IT FEELS TO BE RUN OVER (1900)

It begins with an accident, the inevitable result of ten thousand objects both real and imaginary cosmically tumbling, colliding at the nexus where silver meets secondhand meets skin. The burst of light is the birth of movies.

Before you, a dirt road. A carriage passes, then a cyclist, both stirring a cloud of dust that settles on an automobile. The car is far angrier, making mad S shapes in the road, darting forward like a shark. Logic says move, but you have grown too heavy in this dream and the car is impossibly close. It breaks out of its world into yours, a pharaoh crossing over, a moth errant unto light, and *Oh! Mother* will *be pleased*.

A pause. *Here is death*, an old woman whispers over popcorn. *I knew it would happen like this*. In movies mortality makes your acquaintance, inscripting your bones.

3

A TRIP TO THE MOON (1902)

The eye remembers—at least for an instant. Lucretius called it persistence of vision. Sixteen times a second, each frame sears into the retina just long enough for another to take its place, and *voilà*! The dead come alive.

For Méliès, persistence populated the moon, albeit not with the sturdiest of denizens. Hit a Moonite with your arm, tap him with an umbrella, and poof! Obliterated. A ball of smoke. The same cloud hovered over Star Film Studios when Méliès, watching his fortunes fall, set every reel, every mask, every prop ablaze.

Just to be clear, it's a myth. Not Méliès, nor his fire. Both are real. The eyes. They do not remember, as lovely as it sounds. A rational explanation debunks the theory, makes perfect sense, does well with test audiences. It is reasonable and best ignored, keeping persistence of vision persistent.

Follow the beam. It is a rare kind of monster up there, roaming the moon, ghosting the screen. It is the product of daily sacrifice, where frames sear and claws tear and eyes forget until eventually, the dead just stay dead.

FIGURE 3: Thomas Edison's employees stole early copies of Georges Méliès' movie *A Trip to the Moon* and sold it in America for substantial profits. Méliès was never compensated and was ultimately reduced to selling toys and candy to earn a living.

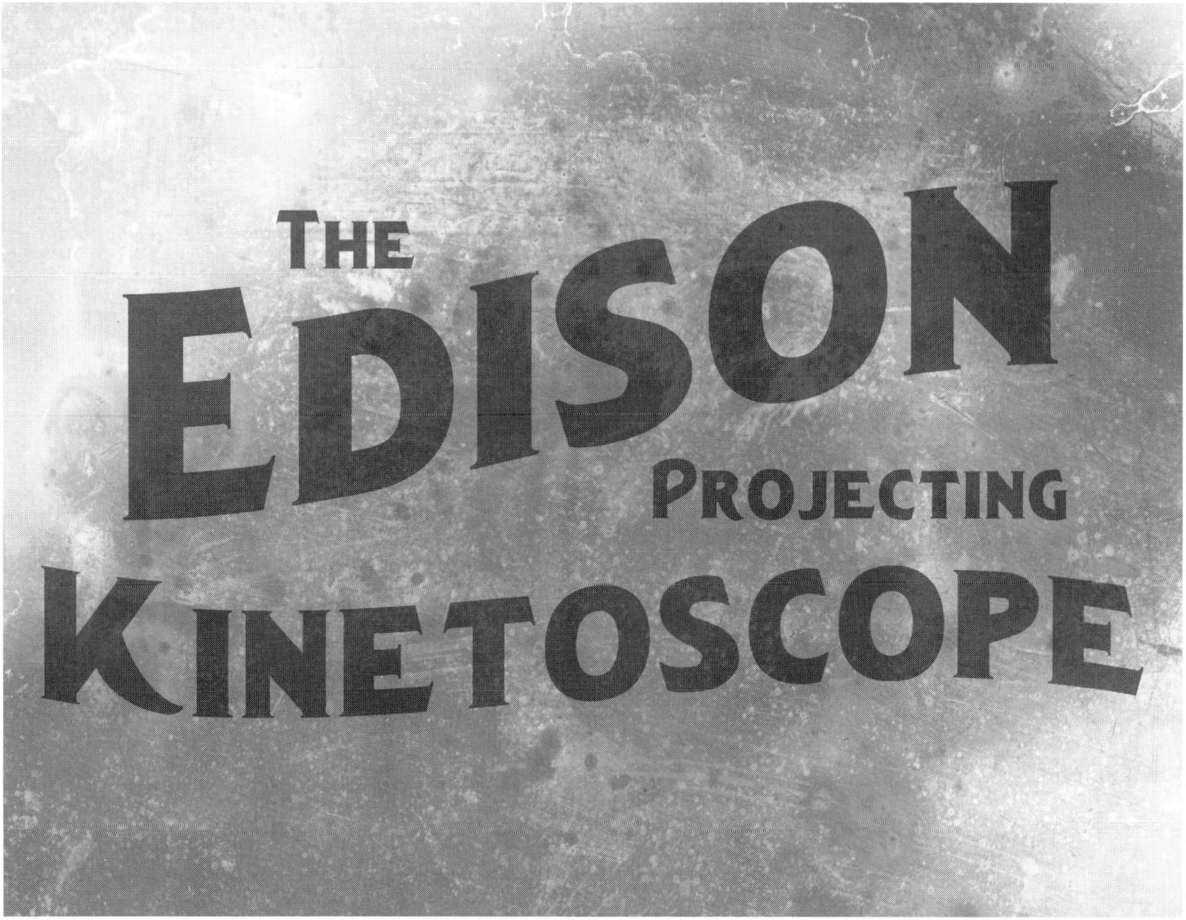

FIGURE 4: In early movies, actors went unnamed.
It was the projector that was the star.

UNCLE JOSH AT THE
MOVING PICTURE SHOW (1902)

Everyone imagines at least one person who is dumber, worse off, or more miserable than they are. It makes daily disasters somehow more bearable.

Edison had Uncle Josh, a fop who thought movies were real, attacking the projectionist when an on-screen farm boy attempts to steal a kiss from Josh's imaginary daughter. *A side-splitter*, Edison says in the catalog, *proof you are not at the bottom of life's totem.*

My family had them as well. The walls echo with *Don't be like your Uncle Delmer*, and the name was enough to scare my father straight. Delmer had a brother named Elmer. Elmer and Delmer. Classic bumblers. Imagine them stepping on rakes, picking fights with mannequins, and poking each other in the eyes. Delmer loved baseball, was hit by an errant slider and died on home plate. It is funny in a clown-car accident kind of way.

Underneath the buffoonery, Uncle Josh gets the final word. The would-be boob knew too well that movies are not part of time but images of time itself, how cats that die in movies haunt us as real cats do. He knew the farm boy could not cover ill-intentions with comedy, and the projectionist, with his pretensions of good clean fun—well, he deserved what he got.

FIGURE 5: Travel is how we practice dying.

THE EUROPEAN REST CURE (1904)

It is the gravity of elsewhere, the Lake Isle of Innisfree, the Boeing gassed on the runway, all pulling all calling all aboard and *au revoir*.

Hearts are not absent, they just hate where they are. And so you take them somewhere else and they hate that too. But the idea of elsewhere is a tidal wave that can be neither resisted nor ridden.

The light flashes on. It isn't the plane, it is the world, dropping. The pilot calls the storm slight turbulence and you say, reassuringly, I've lived a good life, and on the screen inside you're kissing the Blarney Stone, doing Paris, climbing the Alps, one misadventure after the next in Italy, Egypt, and Germany. Everyone has to go some time, you say, because you saw it somewhere and where else can you learn to die if not at the movies.

Thing is, you land. If this is your final destination, there's nowhere else to go. We know you have choices and we are glad you chose us. Beware that luggage might have shifted during the flight and *Life: The Movie* can, but rarely does, end.

For this you are quietly grateful, mildly miserable.

COLLEGE CHUMS (1907)

Our chats, diffused: iPhone bubbles in the cloud. In analog days, text messages hurt as we hurled die-cast letters across immense spaces, putting out an eye or forming a new word. There is no greater sign of love between friends than unabashed vituperation.

Clouds disperse. A volta, unnoticeably slow and unrecognizable until it has passed. Afterwards, new friends are fine, but nothing like old ones, new music swayable, but no longer moving. That which is new appeals the more it alludes to that which is old.

There is little more than loveliness in Márquezian nostalgia. What exists in the past is only this: a well of words poured into pages, the aftermath of soaring letters thrown by college chums I cannot praise enough, a pile of unspeakables that collided mid-air and fell and formed book after book of immeasurable worth.

FIGURE 6: Edwin Porter invented what he called "jumble text," which used stop motion to make text fly across cities.

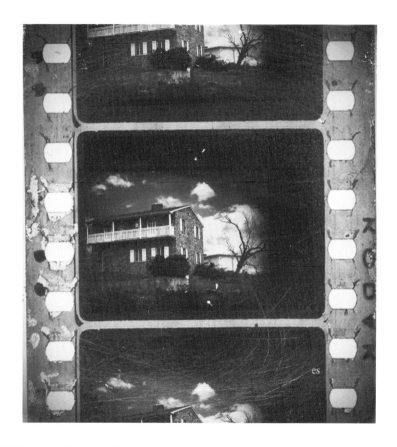

FIGURE 7: *La Maison Ensorcelée* uses no title cards. For many directors, this was an artistic achievement, a form of pure visual storytelling. With *La Maison Ensorcelée*, there is really just not much of a story.

LA MAISON ENSORCELÉE (1908)

Of their own volition, creepy knives cut sausage and stack it neatly. Magic scissors cut hair, magic razors shave chops. Director Segundo de Chomón had a single trick: stop the camera, move something, start it again. It never got old. Segundo was the Ramones of silent comedy.

Over the course of a hundred years, the house of wise-cracking, self-aware objects grows less funny and more unsettled. Ghosts skip beats and travel in bursts, finding horror in the familiar, language in motion.

It explains why my grandfather opened the garage door after his death, why murdered tenants hide keys and move saltshakers. The dead cannot just write you a note. Movement is how they say *This sucks, bring me back.* In the corners of the screen they speak, in flickers and scratches, saying through the darting of our eyes that they are not that far gone.

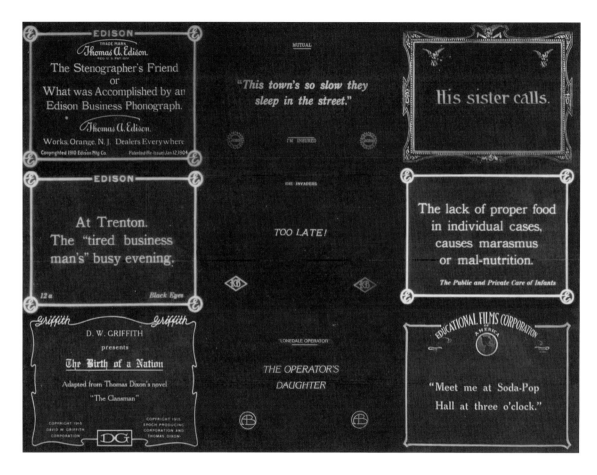

FIGURE 8: In the 1910s, title cards were riddled with company names and logos to thwart would-be thieves. The cards served as both narrative aids and reoccurring copyright notices.

PART II: NARRATIVE CINEMA

In 1910, The Imp Girl died, flattened by a streetcar that jumped the tracks. She had starred in hundreds of short pictures, always taking the name of her studio: The Vitagraph Girl, The Biograph Girl. But The Independent Motion Pictures Girl seemed a little long, hence The Imp Girl.

What happened next is the story of Lazarus or *The Dark Knight Returns*, whichever you prefer. The Imp Girl never died or got near a streetcar. It was a hoax her studio developed to promote *The Broken Oath*, and it worked, even if a typo on the advertisements billed the movie as *The Broken Bath*.

We nail a lie, those fliers stated, *our star is not dead, and if you do not believe it, come see the picture.* People did, en masse, so incredulous of the resurrection that they tore at her clothes. *And just so you are sure this is no joke, her real name is Florence Lawrence.*

After that, there was no more Imp Girl, Biograph Girl, or Vitagraph Girl. There was Florence Lawrence, and everyone knew her. The first real movie star. The Girl with a Thousand Faces.

With the rebirth of Florence came a different kind of movie. In the first part of the century, movies were carnivalesque, all newfangled and ta-da, an amusement park that did not require walking. Florence and the other new names helped shape a different kind of movie, a window to see *through*, to see stars, to see yourself as someone else, an essential part of a vaster tale.

FIGURE 9: Despite his stated dislike of them, D.W. Griffith used 232 title cards in *The Birth of a Nation.*

THE BIRTH OF A NATION (1915)

This is for you. The ushers in Civil War garb, for you. The rows of red velvet cushions, crafted for girdled backs and porcelain bottoms, for you. *The Birth*—a new history formed because you did not like the first one—for you.

A plea. We do not fear censorship, and we demand, as a right, the liberty to show the dark side of wrong, so we might illuminate the bright side of virtue.

We demand it with our hands.

In the quarters of the Majestic, the best boy first saw light under his sheets and found it was his own: thin beams streaming from his palms like light shooting through a pinhole. All over the studio lot, workers woke to the same stigmata, the gaffers, the cutters, the key scenics, and the set designers, waking, wondering, keeping their arms outstretched as if they held fire and wiggling their glowing fingertips as though ready to ascend.

The beams grew stronger by salary and status. The cinematographer: a policeman's flashlight. The director of photography: the light on a freighter's mast.

Just off the lot, still under the storm of luminance, D.W. left a dream to find his palms gone supernova. He reached for his wife in the adjacent bed and cut her in half, along with the wall behind her and the foundation of a neighboring house.

This is the product of those hands, all for you. This palace built for no other purpose, this birth, a world rewritten with lightning, the bright side of virtue slashing the old world to streamers.

A FOOL THERE WAS (1915)

No fear greater
than a woman who wants sex
or who we think wants sex or
who we want to want sex.

(Theda is death rearranged.)

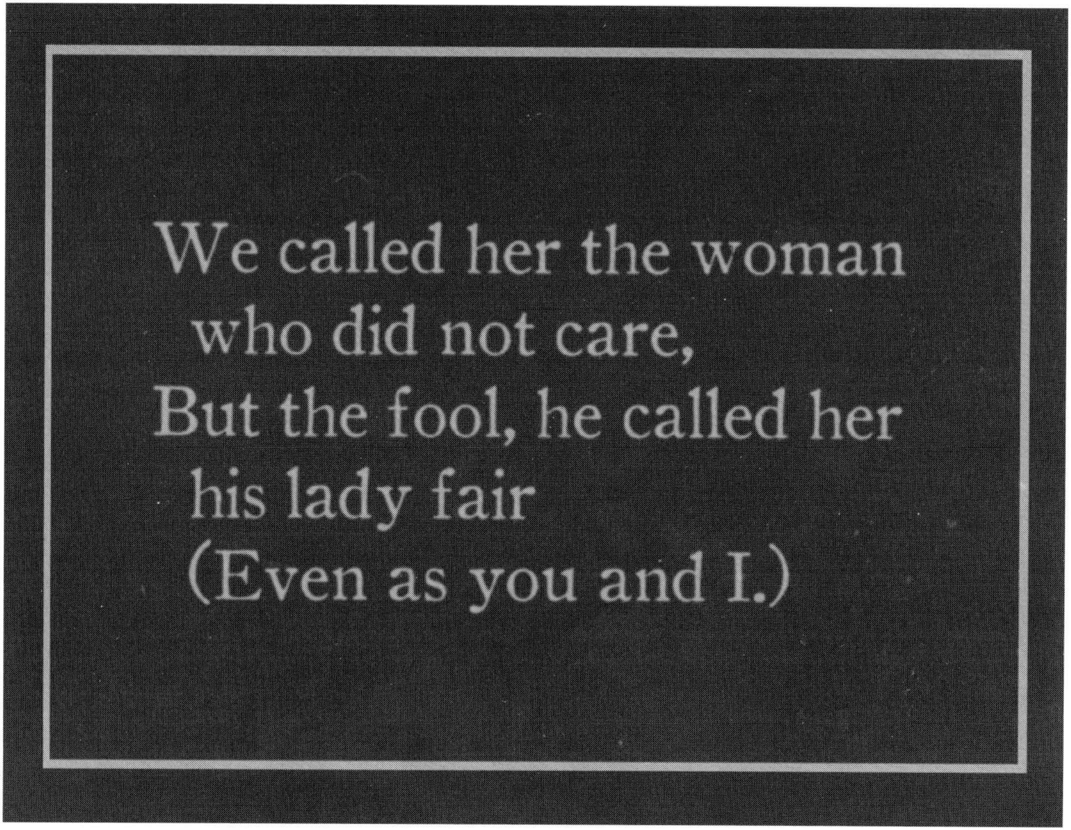

We called her the woman
who did not care,
But the fool, he called her
his lady fair
(Even as you and I.)

FIGURE 10: Theda Bara's *A Fool There Was* uses the
Rudyard Kipling poem "The Vampire" as its foundational text.
It is one of the few silent movies to integrate poetry.

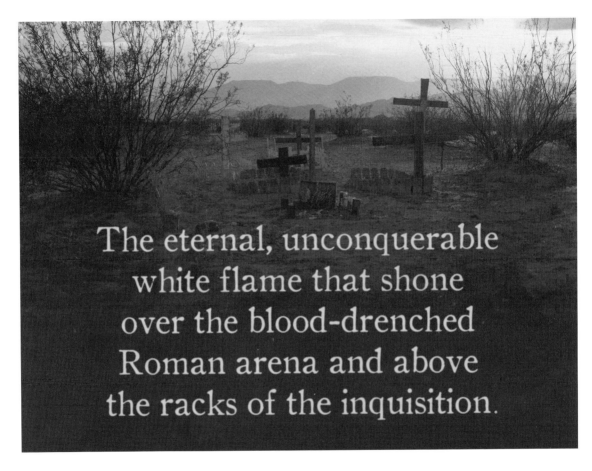

The eternal, unconquerable white flame that shone over the blood-drenched Roman arena and above the racks of the inquisition.

FIGURE 11: The right words turn comedy to horror.

HELL'S HINGES (1916)

When Jennifer Love Hewitt passes ghosts to the next world, grandmothers are always waiting, still knitting, saying, *Come, now, this is the time.* The show's theme song plays, building to crescendo. Walking tentatively towards the light, I tell my grandmother I was a good man, a professor even, deserving of this bliss. She responds, in a voice more haunting than ever, that from her angel's perch she saw me look at porn at work. Porn? Nana, No. Sometimes ads just pop up. Things have changed since—*Insufferable,* she would say. *Our taxes pay for your girlie watching. How can I explain it to the ladies in Heaven's aqua-aerobics? Maybe, dear boy, you should not cross over just yet.*

I imagine Hell as more painful, less embarrassing, horrifically lovely, like the orange fire of burning oil wells in Iraq or the white heat of self-ignited celluloid nitrate. Maybe Satan is not all evil, just more of a jerk, always posting pictures with ironic captions on Hell's Facebook.

Fifteen minutes of sun sears my skin to pomegranate, and reportedly Hell's to-do list is mostly weeping and gnashing of teeth. But there is also openness to change: the gunslinger who finds solace, the woman who finds beauty in coarseness, a desert cat who finds a home. It is where you suffer sincerely, pine, and write, while angels forget how happy they are, lacking any point of comparison.

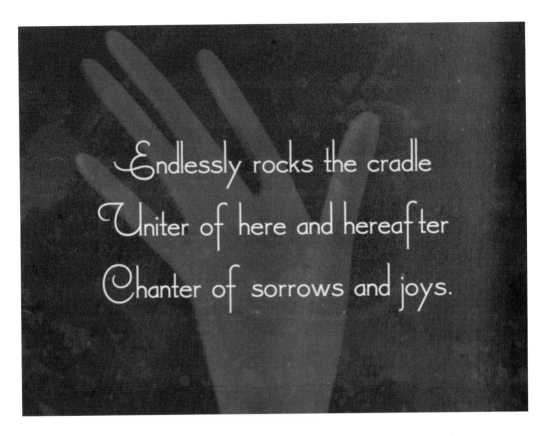

FIGURE 12: An homage to Walt Whitman in Griffith's *Intolerance*.

INTOLERANCE (1916)

Sit over here, Lillian. Yes, in the chair. Place your hand on the cradle and look forlorn. More forlorn than that. I know the lights are hot. Well, of course, but don't you see? It isn't a baby at all, dearest, it is our whole doomed world and you are its mother.

Lillian, I am sorry. Because Mae is already playing that role. No, I gave that one to Miriam. Of course you are still the star. Look, I am not going to—okay, fine, you are much more lovely than Mae. And? Yes, and Miriam too.

Stop? No, you can never stop. You would think, wouldn't you? Maybe it would be more loving to call it quits. But love's real struggle through the ages is ownership, and like it or not, we are yours.

The widening gyre of this world finds solace here, out of the cradle endlessly rocking, and in that space at the center of every doomed life, awkward and unknowing, is the singular certainty of struggle and the shelter of your hands.

FIGURE 13: In *The Mystery of the Leaping Fish*, Douglas Fairbanks stars as a detective who injects bad guys (and himself) with copious amounts of cocaine.

THE MYSTERY OF THE LEAPING FISH (1916)

The mystery is what they see wide-eyed in the post-dart instant when their world is overshot, when the prospect of a nymph is replaced by searing yellow light and a clamping of lungs.

In those blurred snapshots, almost unrecognizable: Fairbanks in a fish floatie, pretending he's Sherlock Holmes. Splash! Browning undressing a flapper with his eyes. Plunk! Griffith sunning himself. Pop! In some ridiculous outfit, absurd even to a fish. Swish! Then the cold, the blue, and slick slide of water and scale.

The mystery is if we would realize if we did the same: broke through, experienced some other world in shards. The mystery is where the fish go that we cannot.

AMERICAN ARISTOCRACY (1916)

The corner lamp glows cobalt and citrine, lighting the bedroom like *Las Meninas*. The far corner, now eclipsed, is no longer space at all, no longer tame and practical.

On screen, it's layer under layer, a secret conference with a mysterious porter, scratched and impossible to discern. Something happens in that darkness. Notes are exchanged, plans are made. It is nefarious no doubt, but a lily in a crystal nonetheless.

A bleached photo of an unlabeled home, tea green with a gray birch in front, tucked in with the family artifacts of weddings and vacations. No one recognizes it, but I wake there sometimes, stepping out to the porch and greeting the sun.

Marry me. Let clarity and precision live with kings and queens who cannot let go, who command the world with wall-mounted landscapes and *trompe l'oeil*. The other world is ours, yours and mine, this hazy kingdom of silent film and forgotten Polaroids.

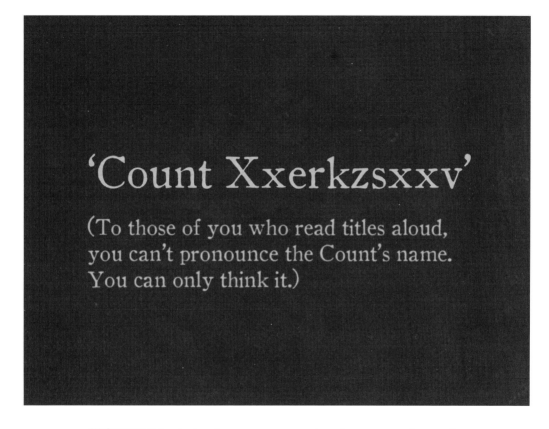

'Count Xxerkzsxxv'

(To those of you who read titles aloud,
you can't pronounce the Count's name.
You can only think it.)

FIGURE 14: Anita Loos wrote seriously sassy title cards.
She was one of the first professional title writers and she
often spoke directly to the audience.

BROKEN BLOSSOMS, OR THE YELLOW MAN AND THE GIRL (1919)

So many bodies, drifting like white blood cells in the in-between where people only go on the way to something else.

I am grateful I do not know you, grateful for crowds of petals on a wet black whatever.

Imagine Death distracted, lost in nostalgia, watching Netflix or momentarily dazzled as the hidden spirit of beauty breaks her blossoms all about his chamber.

This is when you get away with it: texting while driving through school zones, pretending you are Stallone in *Cliffhanger*, wondering about finally swallowing that quarter. You can hear the cello moan as the blossom secretly drops and dying no longer seems abstract.

But you live. And what makes this meaningful is not the realization of some cosmic order or a zest for life, but that it will be a stranger who saves you, a petal in the crowd, and she will wander away and stay a stranger.

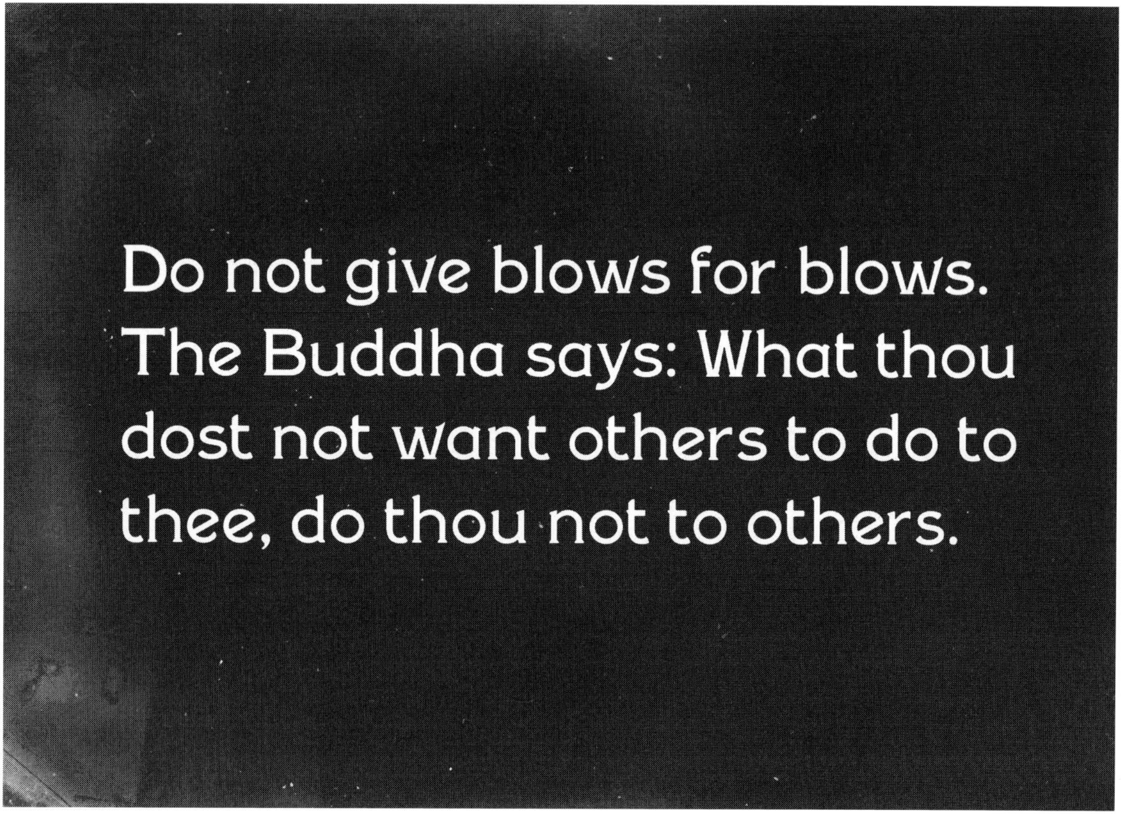

FIGURE 15: After *The Birth of a Nation*, D.W. Griffith's movies had an oft-repeated theme: Sorry for *The Birth of a Nation*.

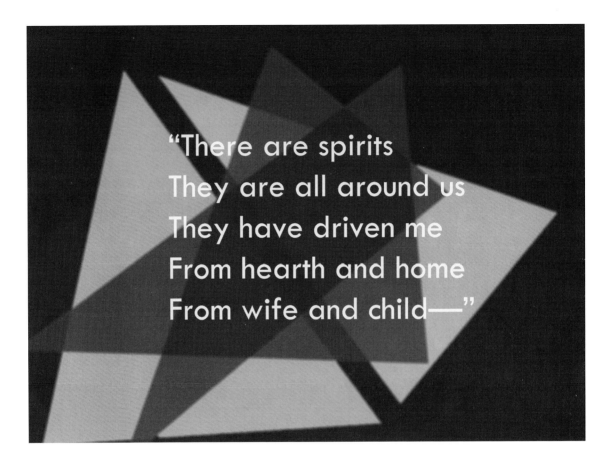

FIGURE 16: If there were an award for creepy title cards, the German Expressionists would win.

THE CABINET OF DR. CALIGARI (1920)

Write this down, Francis. You haven't much time for error.

You rent your life from a landlord with a stained undershirt he wears each day with no overshirt. He is fat, mustachioed, and clean-domed. He runs your body on the single principle that it is easier to drool over running shoes than to go out and run. Over his desk there is a sign with letters branded black into red oak:

Not what you want. What you want right now.

It takes years to learn what you must learn in minutes: To feel anything you have to trash the place like a sophomore who drank away his student loans. It's Buddhism 101. The carpet is your skin, the cabinet your center. Both have to sail out the window and lie in the courtyard, so people can wonder what the hell happened up there, unaware that you are no longer of this world.

Write this down, Francis. You do not even make it the whole 71 minutes.

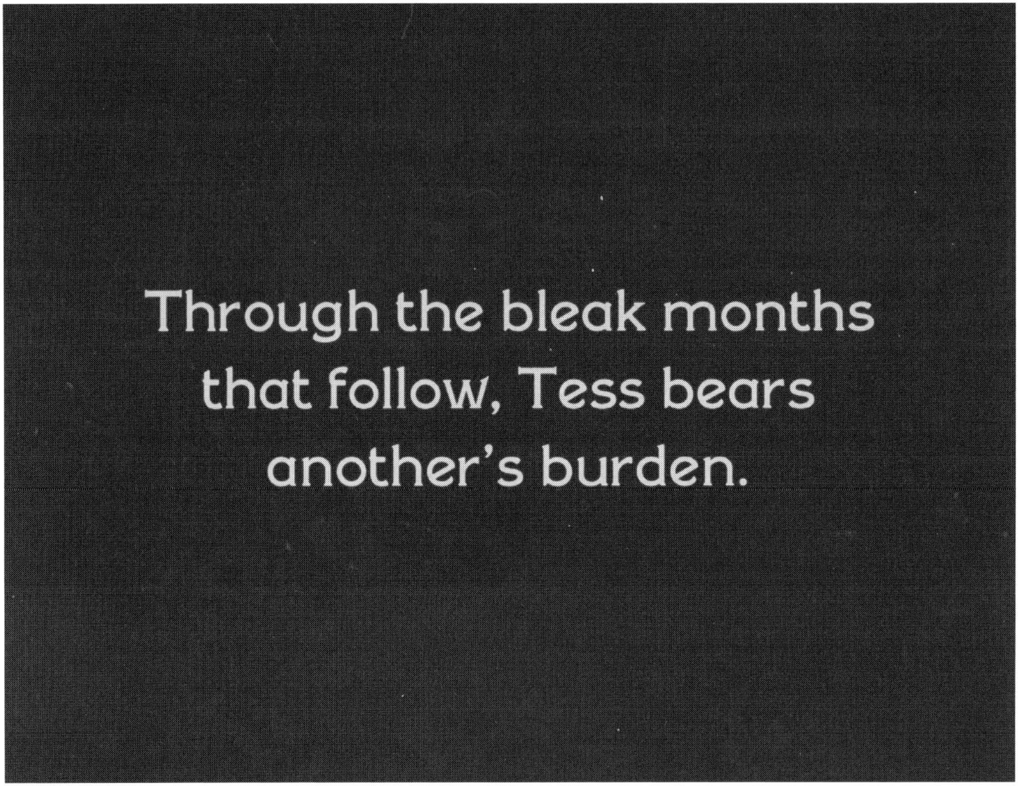

FIGURE 17: According to G.E. Lessing,
text operates in time, images in space.

TESS OF THE STORM COUNTRY (1922)

Invisible oceans of warm and cold air collide, turning cobalt and blocking the sun. Tess raises her arms—what comes next lets us live.

Elias loves Orn because Orn is poor and Elias needs poor people to clarify what he is not. Elias' language of love is shaking fists and harrumphing until his monocle falls loose and he is forced to retrieve it.

Orn loves Elias too, though he would never admit it. Elias is confusing and distant, right on the edge of actually living. Orn pities him, but when Elias comes to visit, Orn always has a shotgun in hand.

Tess raises her arms. She is a cloud, born to shelter, hold, and break apart, to stand impossibly between these two foes. She sees the secret between them, their deep mutual affection, and knows it is how the world works, that no enmities are forgotten in another's need, just redirected, sent upwards, crashing into the cold air and sending down the rain.

THE SEA HAWK (1924)

One of the many advantages of befriending scoundrels is the ease with which I can envision myself more holy. Yet I always envy them as well—for sleeping in until two, for devoting their days to video games and anime, for partners who find this recalcitrance irresistible.

Perhaps it is the musk of a swashbuckler that lives by steel and falcon, a spirit that does not fade when his new conquest must start paying his credit card bills. Breathe in the reckless audacity. On a wooden ship under a black flag, a man feels something compelling and unspeakable leading towards the horizon. He finds a girl, kidnaps her, and sells her into slavery, concurrently declaring his love. He buys her at the last minute with money he stole, then makes her his wife.

It's easy to blame, but hard to explain, these modern pirates, ever lured towards bolder horizons, and perhaps the same inexplicable drive draws others to them, to make for them homes, dinners, and allowances.

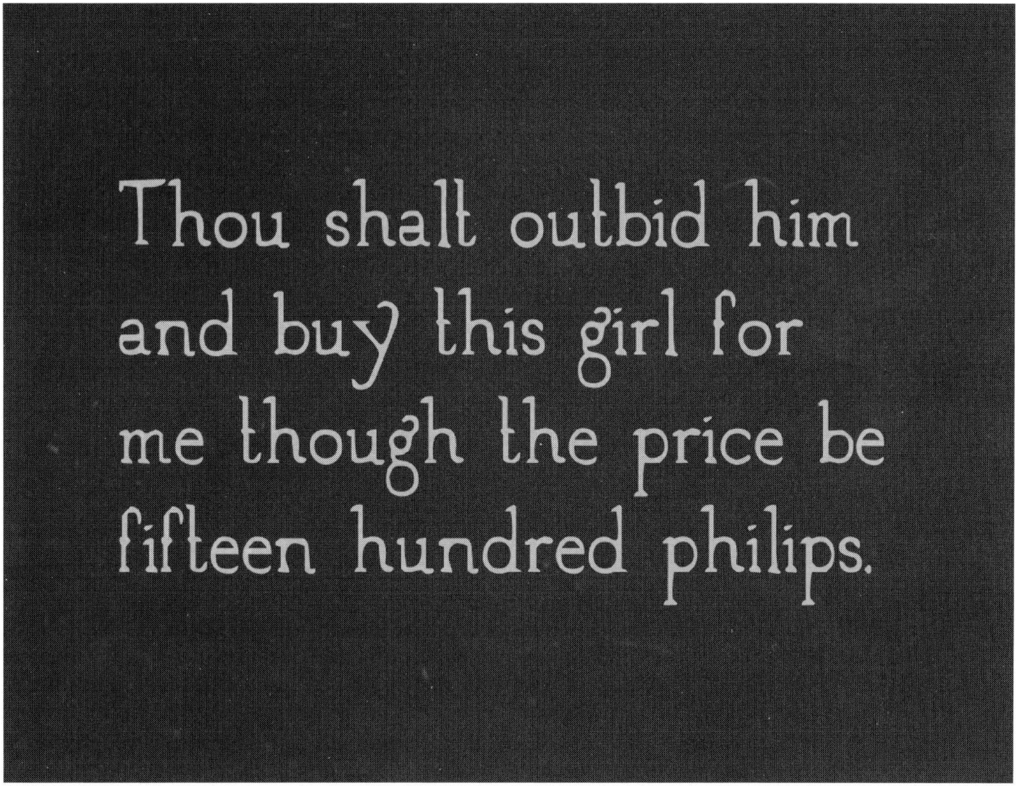

Thou shalt outbid him
and buy this girl for
me though the price be
fifteen hundred philips.

FIGURE 18: In Hollywood's biggest film library, only one title card exists. It is not this one. It is from a 1926 movie called *The Cave Man*, which has been lost or destroyed.

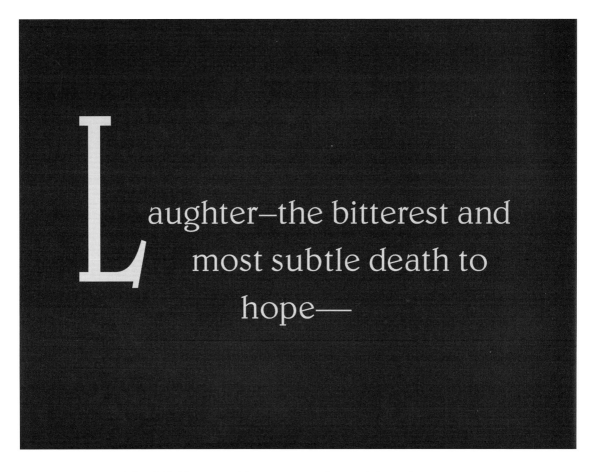

Laughter–the bitterest and most subtle death to hope—

FIGURE 19: Lon Chaney wins for saddest clown ever.

HE WHO GETS SLAPPED (1924)

Every clown needs a shtick. Paul's was to get slapped when he said something smart. Drunk with *schadenfreude*, the crowd begged for more, for Aristotle, Rousseau.

Zen monks seem agreeable, even comic, until they thwap you with a cane. The pain is a window, how they help you stop seeing and start *seeing through*.

A man with eyes unnaturally blue honed his anger as a third-grade teacher and a mixed martial artist. When my face met his glove then the canvas, my grandmother spoke to me.

Paul finds no answers in hundreds of slaps, then dies. Best not to watch Lon Chaney movies if you want easy answers.

The Zen alternative to enlightenment through beating is a koan, a question with no answer. They open windows too, but slowly, and people have appointments to keep so most choose the cane.

Stop throwing rocks at your cousins, my grandmother said. Traveling from beyond the grave, having only seconds to whisper something profound in my ear, this was the best she could do.

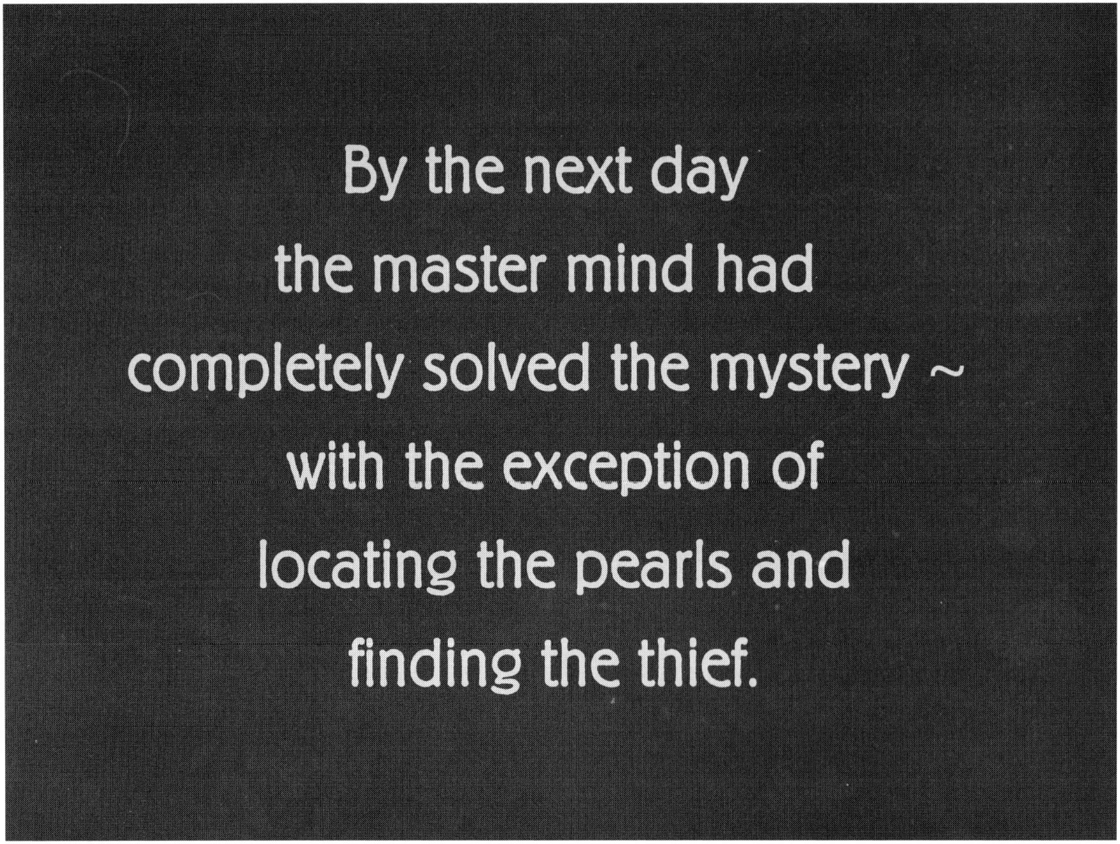

By the next day
the master mind had
completely solved the mystery ~
with the exception of
locating the pearls and
finding the thief.

FIGURE 20: In context, this is crazy funny.

SHERLOCK, JR. (1924)

Chapter 1: Your goal as a detective is to find the edges of the known world and to learn of your karmic connection with every crime. Any great detective will tell you the trick is not walking into movies but finding the way out again.

Chapter 2: Detectives know that the walls holding back an unthinkable zoo of experience have fallen to dust. Free now are first kisses to rub noses with failed tests, divorce papers to fight and be flung at family reunions, and first cars to crash and consider and heal at last upon the final words of a wedding or funeral. There is no rebuilding this fortress of nostalgia.

Chapter 3: Cases are never solved, but that is your great secret, because you may transcend time and space but you still need a paycheck, and the only thing worse on a payroll than a psychotic butler is an existentialist detective.

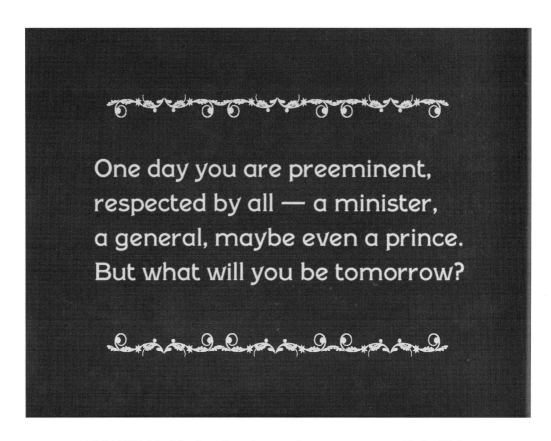

One day you are preeminent,
respected by all — a minister,
a general, maybe even a prince.
But what will you be tomorrow?

FIGURE 21: *The Last Laugh* was the precursor to *Fight Club*, questioning the link between identity and occupation.

THE LAST LAUGH (1924)

When I was sixteen, McDonald's did not call me back, even to say no. The sweaty-browed manager instinctively knew I was not McDonald's material.

Burger King took me in with the grace of a neglected mom, and put me beside Glen, who had stolen a lawnmower not once but thrice and now had a lopsided back tattoo of a skull. He said "thrice" sometimes, incorrectly, as in *I will thrice make your Double Whopper*. The manager deemed burger making too complicated for me and believed my true potential would blossom by putting things in fryers and pulling them out.

For joy, Mr. Sarcastic in the Drive Thru, I messed with your food. The last laugh is mine.

You are not your job, but there are no dividing lines in the soul. For whatever I am, I am also Burger King and Di Nappoli Pizza, Ponderosa Steak House and grocery stores and bookstores and café sinks filled with dishes. I am a human sign for companies with inexcusable indifference to human suffering.

They hold corporate picnics in my brain, talking teamwork, synergy, and washing hands not once but thrice.

THE RED KIMONA (1925)

The flies that cover his body are in Heaven. For them, the great beyond is a rotting place, with people to annoy and without rolled up newspapers.

One has to wish that regret crossed his mind before the bullet did: *I am sorry I took you to New Orleans and sold you into prostitution. It seemed like the right move at the time.*

Or that sadness plagued the old woman that traded you shelter for social status: *Dearie, I had no idea. My inner altruism came alive by highlighting your inner whore. But tell me, before I die, do they pay you more for, you know, [an inaudible whisper].*

The world balances in many ways, but not this one. Our all-inclusive Hippie Heaven does not discriminate. They are all there, the ones who thrived on your suffering or were simply indifferent to it. The man you loved and trusted is there, flittering about, harp in hand, doing what he loves best:

Taking young girls to New Orleans and selling them into prostitution.

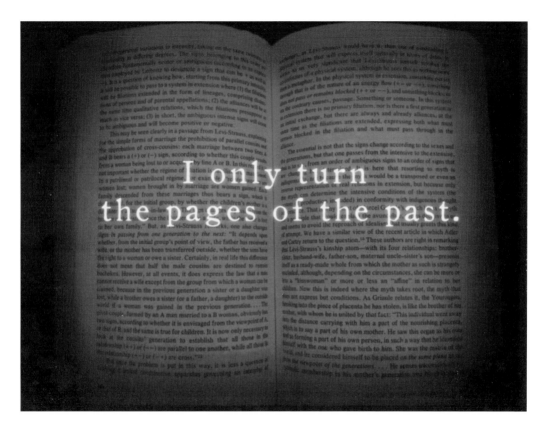

FIGURE 22: Silents sometimes began with a shot of a book opening as a way of linking the images to a literary source and the authority that connection entailed.

THE GENERAL (1926)

Speeding steam-powered, the question of collision is not if but when and how the hell am I going to fix this one.

There are two loves in my life, train A and train B, careening towards each other across continents. If it were not for their constant promise of disaster and repair, I do not know why I would bother to wake. I miss them when they are gone, these trains without brakes, without plans, and ultimately without rails. There is a joy in crisis, the possibility of being useful, noticed.

There were two
Loves in his life
His engine
And

The elation of near misses,

where planet and asteroid, single prop and mountain, the car, the driver on his cell, the ball, the child who chases it where the world bends at the brink of their union, and the two veer and slide past, each overwhelmed by their perfect proximity.

Once our trains and troops cross that bridge, nothing on earth can stop us.

FIGURE 23: Things do not end well for this bridge.

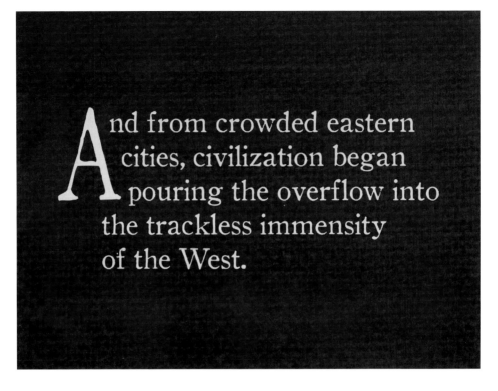

FIGURE 24: Critics sometimes referred to titles as being of the "rosy-fingered dawn" style if the writing was overly sentimental or dramatic. It was an epithet borrowed from Homer's *Odyssey*.

3 BAD MEN (1926)

I am going to ruin it for you. All three die, shot repeatedly or blown to *polvo* in a shed full of dynamite.

In a young girl who drifts like heat in the Mojave they find time for revision and a glimpse at their own demise.

For Frank Kermode, storytellers are apocalyptic prophets, predicting and preparing an end then rescheduling once the fateful date passes and we're all still here. Where was Moses when the lights went out? We imagine a world like this, only better. The apocalyptic trick is to bend trust without breaking it, to lead by the hand rather than by the wrist.

One early morning, I looked out the front door and saw blood, small dark drops, crimson and thick. Coming closer, I found a trail, leading down the sidewalk, past the rosemary, behind the laurel tree, and through the begonias. The trail grew bolder as it rounded a corner, small pools blackened by the morning sun, ending at the neighbor's gate. Reaching up slowly, I unfastened the latch, slid the door open and

But you already know what is there.

The void swallows all light except that which is projected upon it. It is why post-death fantasy is a world so much like this one only better, why the three bad men who sacrifice themselves for youth come back again, for the last few seconds, tipping hats in the sunset and riding again into the rosy-fingered blur of the Mojave.

Der Traum
(the dream)

FIGURE 25: Freud was mostly ambivalent towards movies, despite their role as our collective dreams.

SECRETS OF A SOUL (1926)

Nine out of 10 men do not want to get jacked up on coke then sleep with their moms. One out of 10 does, and that is why there are movies.

Psychoanalysis has nothing to do with coke or mom-banging. Sorry. It might be more fun if it did. Forgotten to most is the all-out wonder of a boy who sees a path and believes it never-before discovered. Imagine Sigmund saying *Come with me, I have unlocked the secret of dreams.*

What you want you cannot have and that makes you want it more. And what you want is not what you think. *Dreams,* Sigmund said, *are not stories at all, even the ones where you talk to chipmunks who tell you to kill.* Not stories at all, but hieroglyphs, some ancient self communicating to you in modernist verse. You do not have to understand it. You just have to say it. Again and again you say it because that is what your wants want, for you to acknowledge that you are one giant factory of the absurd.

The secret of your soul is that you are a mess trying to pull it all together, boxing multitudes into a single home. Sigmund dreamed himself an explorer of this Borgesian structure, where he could follow winding halls and spiral steps leading nowhere, and claim the last undiscovered territory as his own.

NINE STAR TITLE WRITERS

By MALCOLM STUART BOYLAN.

NINE men of assorted waist-lines, accents and origins, are titling practically all of the big pictures with which Hollywood entertains, or enrages 20,000,000 people every evening.

Just what is a title writer, and why are there only nine of importance?

An embarrassing question, indeed, for one of the self-appointed dignitaries!

Angeles newspaper man before his particular flair for brilliant comedy made him famous as a screen dialoguist.

John W. Krafft of the De Mille studios was also a newspaper man and had written considerable magazine stuff before his entry into the films.

The industry today would be glad to pay $50,000 a year apiece to twenty title writers. There is a place for

FIGURE 26: The nine were masters of curt phrasing. They had all started as newspaper men, where every word had to matter.

PART III: THE END OF SILENTS

In 1927, Warner Brothers produced *The Jazz Singer*, the first major movie to feature synchronized sound. The number of silents plummeted for the next three years, and by 1931, they had been replaced almost entirely by the talkies.

During this time, as silents became increasingly unpopular, nine men met every week for lunch. They called themselves the Titular Bishops. As silent movies had grown more complex, studios had hired them to write title cards. The right words at the right place could transform anything. You would think these might be gloomy meetings. Like lamplighters before them and bookstore employees after, technology replaced their services. But by at least two accounts, these were the most riotously funny lunches one could hope to attend. The nine drank excessively, bagged on one another, and told more jokes than anyone could absorb, all of them good. At these lunch parties, they let an era go, and shifted their concerns to tomorrow's hangover.

Ralph Spence, the famous title writer and dream traveler, was always at the head of this table. But now, after barging into another dream, he does not like to talk about it. *I get it*, he says, *nothing lasts. But it is hard to get untangled from silver and nostalgia.* He says he is more movie than dream. When he gets this way, I try to change the topic. If I do not, he tends to disappear when I turn away, and I am never entirely sure when he will come back.

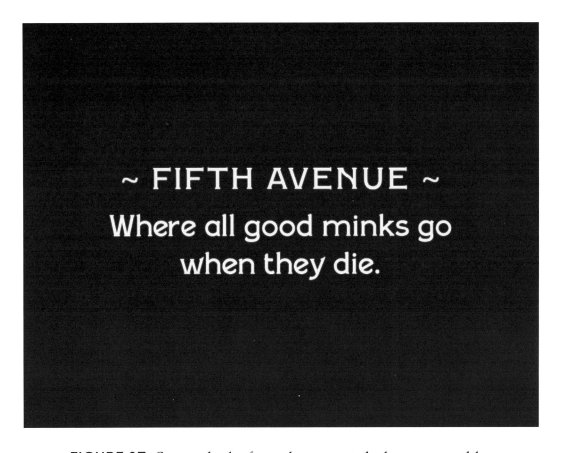

~ FIFTH AVENUE ~
Where all good minks go
when they die.

FIGURE 27: Spence had a formula—a straight line, some tildes, and then an ironic line. His job was to write them and insert them at just the right moment.

ORCHIDS AND ERMINE (1927)

O, they are lovely, the eyes that pine.

The telephone operator with bobbed black hair resting her head on her hands and her elbows on her desk, eyes on the glass door, dreaming of elsewhere.

The ex-prince, thin from fasting, under a tree where temptations blow in like leaves, his eyes fixed on the darkness, wanting so much not to want.

She thinks of a boy with money to take her away, of flowers and furs, real orchids, real ermine. Da Vinci painted Cecilia Gallerani with one. They turn cake-white in the winter and will stop your world upon encounter in a snowy field, and there is nothing more horrible than turning one into a scarf.

Nothing more horrible, that is, except wishing those wishes away, nothing else to call it but hating the world. There is too little time to suffer, to pine, to feel unfulfilled, too many possible lives in her elsewhere eyes.

Golf was invented by the Dutch in an effort to make the Scotch forget bagpipes.

FIGURE 28: Title writers were often called "gag men" even if they were not very funny.

SPRING FEVER (1927)

Unspoken is the hidden terror of golf, its potential to obliterate us all when the density of life lessons reaches critical mass and implodes into a void so dense that even the smallest blade of grass cannot escape.

Ease up and let the club do the work. It is a game of hits and misses. A good bounce here and a bad one there make all the difference.

Can you feel the momentum building?

Justin Timberlake, harassed by a reporter from the *Times*, says golf is about accepting one's own heart of darkness and realizing the futility of human endeavor. "Tempo is everything in music," he says. "I see a correlation to golf."

There is no correlation, and his clichés pull soul from center. Perhaps words really can kill, as they do in *Dune*. Perhaps when I say *play the ball as it lies* as a metaphor for dealing with given circumstances, a kitten in China dies.

Joan Crawford plays golf in heels. It is what they did in the 20s, but even so, her swing makes onlookers inexplicably sad.

Arnold Palmer says that what other people may find in poetry or art museums, he finds in the flight of a good drive.

TILLIE THE TOILER (1927)

There is something that loves a wall, some unacknowledged joy in resisting the path of least resistance. It is the part of the brain that prays for crisis, for car wrecks, and the life-changing disasters that come in the nick of time.

There is something that does not love an open road.

Enter Tillie, with two pairs of garters. One to hold up her stockings, the other to hold up traffic. The moment she tilts her head, sighs, says something coy as her hand lingers too long—can she be loved turns to can she be tamed and men learn who they are is not who they want to be.

It is no secret. There are easier choices, easier bedfellows, and a singular certainty—it will not end well.

You know this before you start, but do it anyway.

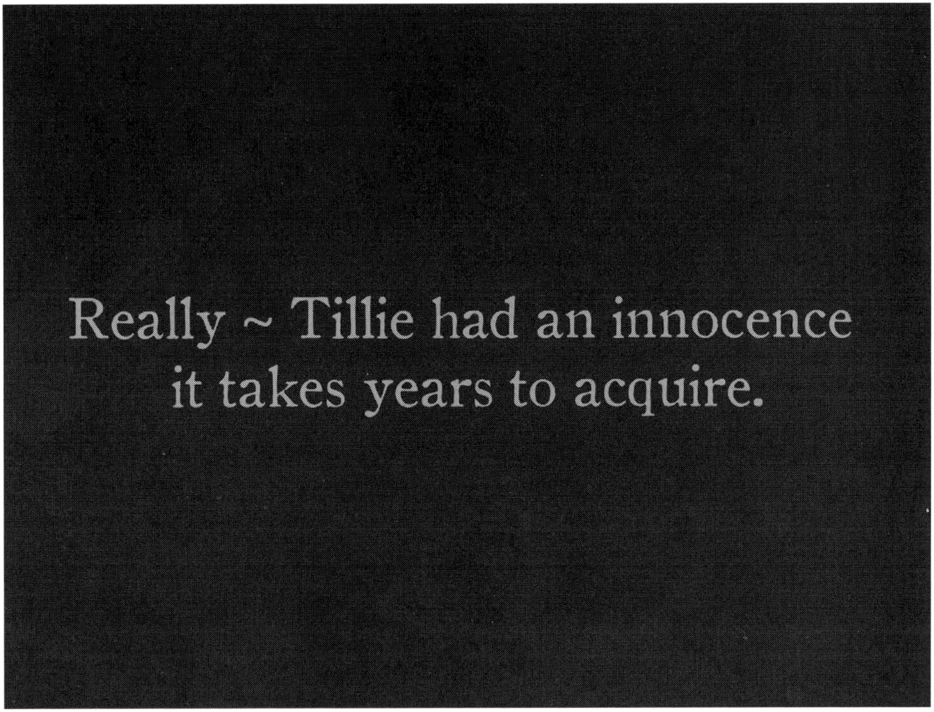

Really ~ Tillie had an innocence
it takes years to acquire.

FIGURE 29: Once I drove six hours to dig around a cemetery to find
Ralph Spence's grave, crossing state and vastly darker lines.

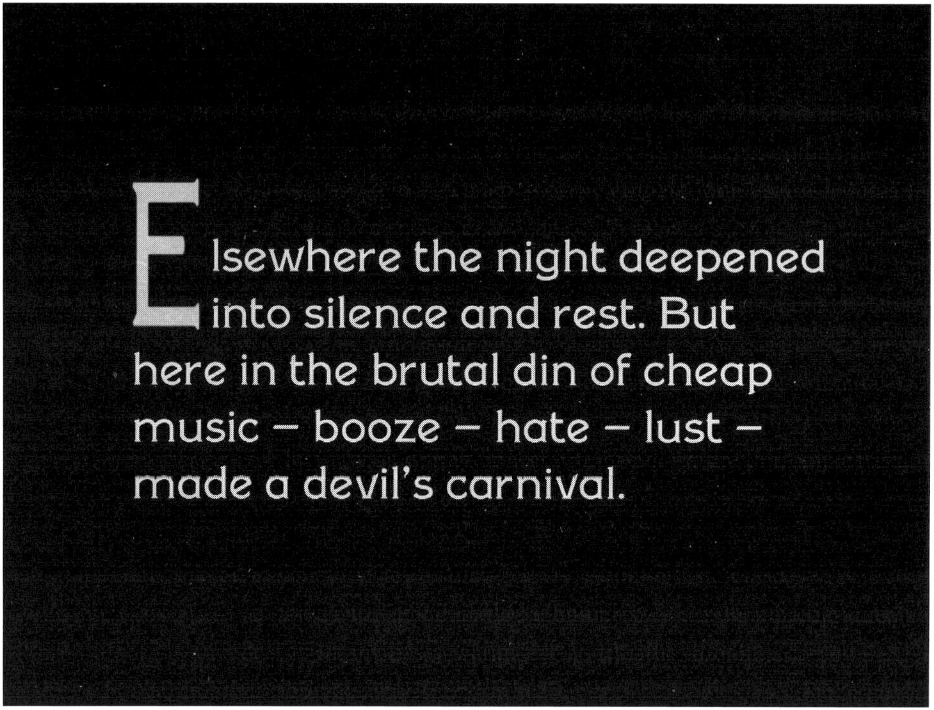

Elsewhere the night deepened into silence and rest. But here in the brutal din of cheap music – booze – hate – lust – made a devil's carnival.

FIGURE 30: There was a rumor in Hollywood that producers would bring George Marion, Jr. a full movie with all the scenes completed, but they would not know if it was a comedy or a drama until Marion had written the titles.

UNDERWORLD (1927)

There is an aesthetics to trespassing, a beauty in being where you should not.

Not old enough to know any better, I waded through a pool of boards and rusty nails to sneak into an abandoned hospital with narrow halls and holes in the floors. There were signs of recent life in the rooms—bedrolls and old magazines. Glass broke on the floor below and my flashlight flickered and died. Fumbling for the dim light of a window, the sound of glass settling turned to voices.

Outside, a great city in the dead of night: streets lonely, moon-flooded. The bar was called Sneakers. After four a.m., it is a perfect void, filled with empty booths and denizens that turn the world into a film noir. Drink and smoke deliberately—the end of hope greeted with alacrity.

Easy, here, to get used to staring forward. There is a cemetery outside of town, unofficial and unmarked. People bury their pets there, fencing off tiny plots, visiting and bringing bones to set on their graves. If you are worthy, a white cat will follow you around. Her way of saying *You shouldn't be here, but I am glad nevertheless.*

SUNRISE (1927)

The trick is not to trick a fish at all. Better to offer him something so impossibly good that all reason fails.

Darting out before supper he chases a lure, the flicker outside all known worlds that looks perfectly obtainable in this one. In a dark pool beyond the trees, he finds her like a sunrise, bobbed hair that curls in double barbs about her cheeks. He springs and she flees—caught, she kicks her legs and giggles, his arms around her waist.

An old fish will tell you with his eyes that the trick is to go back into thick wood, where the line will get tangled and break. But there is a reason they aren't all old fish.

He pauses, bites his lip, and tastes something unexpectedly metallic: *And my wife?*

The head of a number #18 Black Ghost can glisten irresistibly in the moonlight and there is no time to think things through. She has only to tilt slightly and let the moon fill her eyes: *Couldn't she get drowned?*

No breaking the line now. Younger fish will fight and die with a blank look, but older ones, after all tricks have failed, seem to realize something. They turn on their side at the end and simply give up.

With their eye towards the vast blue screen, it is how they curse desire.

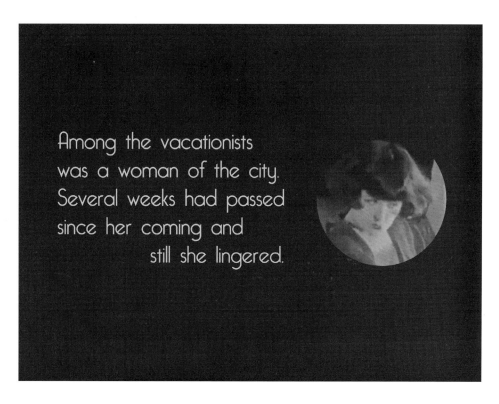

Among the vacationists was a woman of the city. Several weeks had passed since her coming and still she lingered.

FIGURE 31: In *Sunrise,* a man tries to drown his wife. Then they have a fun day in the city and she forgives him. It happens, I suppose, more than we would like to imagine.

THE LODGER (1927)

The founding myth is that people fled from the theaters upon seeing a movie of a train coming towards them. The story survives because present people like to think themselves smarter than past people. Whatever happened, the train made no subtle entry into our world. It was the cousin just out of prison or the college kid unable to find a job. Like it or not, I am home. I could always crash on the couch.

When barging in failed, movies found their way around to the front door, sneaking in side windows, fedoras, and Happy Meals. They manifested like ghosts, setting up residence and leaving false memories. Joel Black calls them kernel truths, persuasive testaments to the idea that something is or was, even if it is not or was not.

The trick to a happy life is to imagine a movie for which you have already seen the end, one that leaves you breathless. Then work backwards to today. Whatever horror, whatever elation, it all leads to that known conclusion.

I learned to kiss from movies, to lie, to move to an imaginary soundtrack. The strange visitors have lodged in so many uncharted nodes that I can no longer evict them.

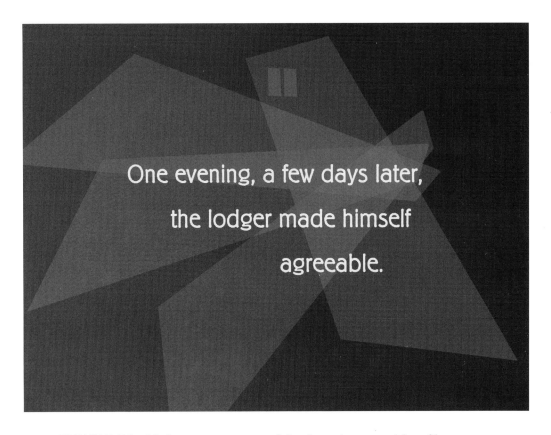

One evening, a few days later, the lodger made himself agreeable.

FIGURE 32: Unknown to most, Hitchcock started his film career writing title cards, as did Herman "Mank" Mankiewicz, the screenwriter of *Citizen Kane*.

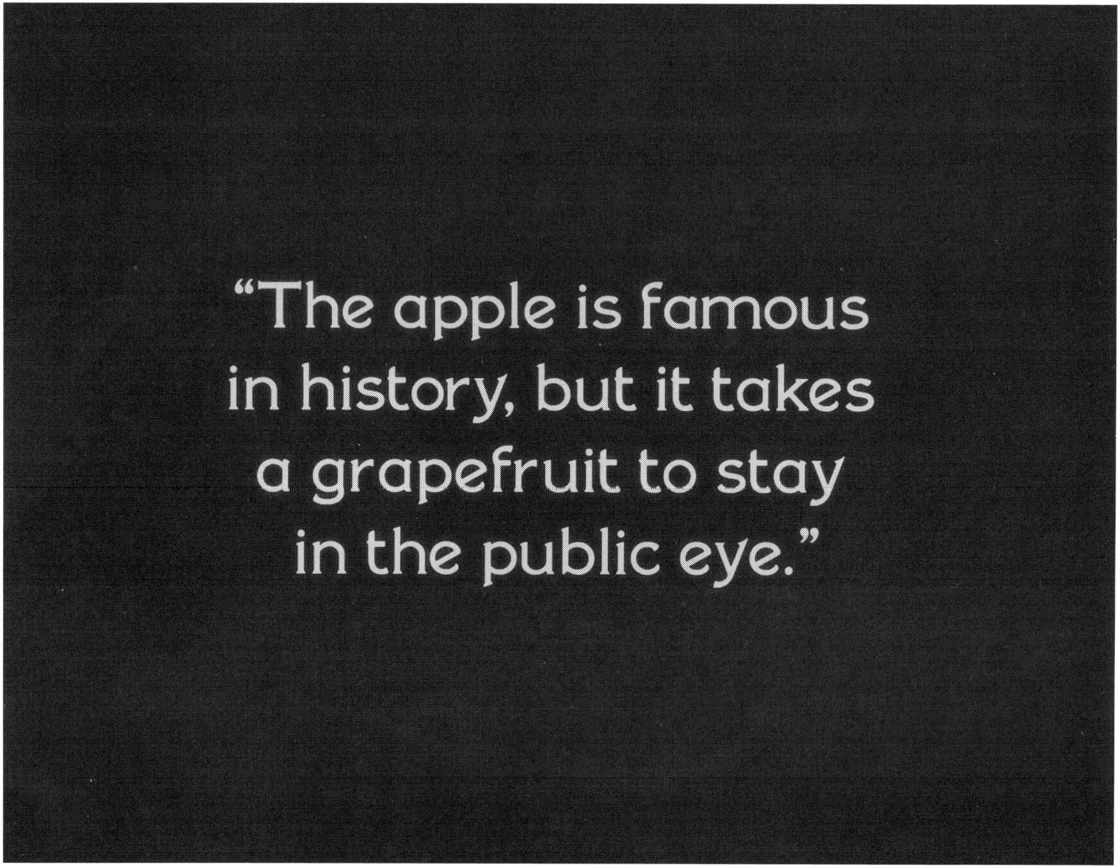

"The apple is famous in history, but it takes a grapefruit to stay in the public eye."

FIGURE 33: Actors often do not say what their cards report. Hilarity ensues.

THE PATSY (1928)

Marion arches her lips, wrinkles her nose, and morphs into Mae Murray.

Nature gives us many of our features, but she lets us pick our own teeth.

To contain multitudes sounds like hyperbole, but the real stretch is to think there is only one, that the you hitting snooze every morning is not a bunch of you, all terrified of waking and meeting one another.

There is always a backup you.

Marion drops her lips, folds her eyes, and becomes Lillian Gish.

And all of you are growing too, learning and evolving, so that even if you could know all their names it wouldn't matter. This army of you always rebels, telling itself next year, I will be better.

But before next year comes, Lillian Gish is Pola Negri, and waiting turns to wanting once more.

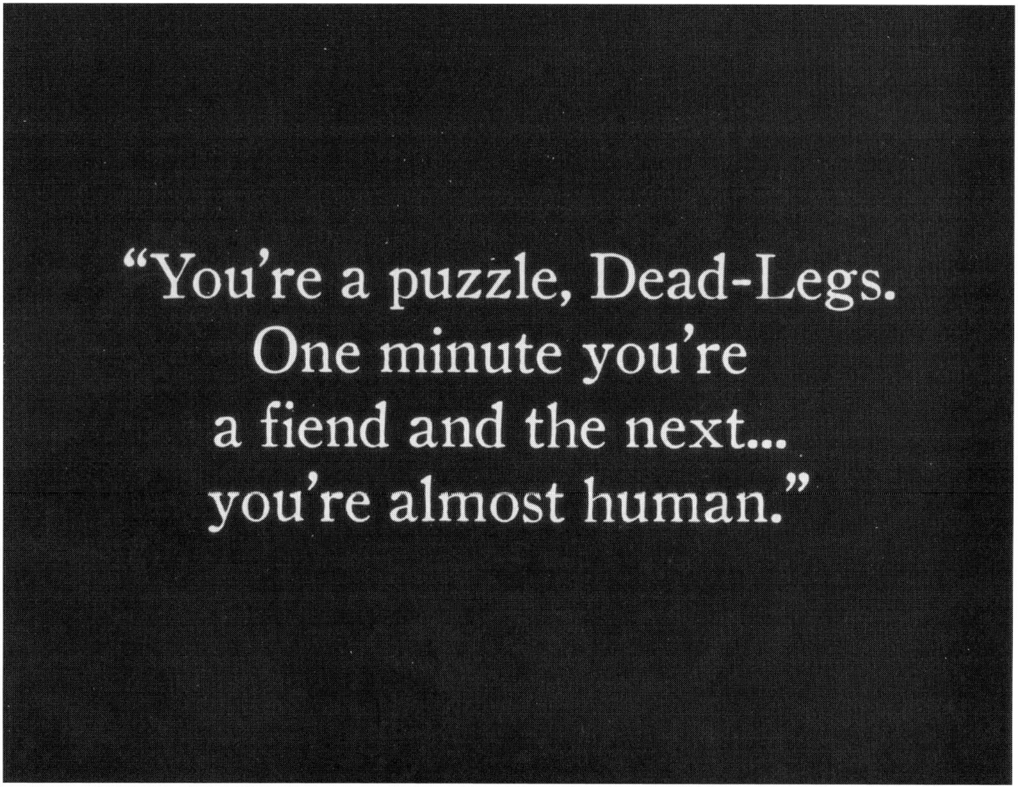

"You're a puzzle, Dead-Legs.
One minute you're
a fiend and the next...
you're almost human."

FIGURE 34: Lon Chaney wins your heart
through his constant thirst for revenge.

WEST OF ZANZIBAR (1928)

There is no getting even, no settling of cosmic scores. When all enemies are vanquished, an even greater emptiness takes hold, a void even more difficult to inhabit.

Phroso woke with limbs rather than legs, never to walk again. Gone too, his wife and friend, but gained was a newfound ability to wait and plan and crawl. Arm over arm, as years turn to decades, he pulls his torso along deadly trails in the heart of the jungle, smoldering, mapping each detail of the path that must lead them back to him. In their final meeting, in their crippling sorrow, he imagines feeling his legs again.

It is an impossible but well-trodden path, where selfishness transforms to sacrifice. But the moral does little to negate the *jouissance*, the eyes that savor the chance of the world made right again, debts paid, solace granted. Not outside this dark room, of course, but in here, yes. The sweetness is palatable. Revenge is a dish best served in courses, relished like Procne watching her husband eat their child.

SHOW PEOPLE (1928)

Erving Goffman calls it giving out as opposed to just giving. It is the life projected rather than the life as is.

In the mirror every morning, I practice moods:

Passion (head forward, eyes slightly askew)
Anger (tilt back, tighten lips)
Sorrow (close like a burgundy curtain)
Joy (open like the buttons on a blue dress)

It is all a matter of practice.

Practice, because there is always a mirror, and the days are silver and three-key lit, and long before movies, when weeks became reels became worlds, you were perfect. A star.

With ten or twenty years of meditation, you can see every breath for what it is, as if your mind is the screen. Objective, outside, above. But for whatever peace this brings, and whatever cycles of birth and rebirth it ends, how could your feet not miss cool soil, how could your tongue not miss apples and salt, how could brown eyes not miss the lure of blue.

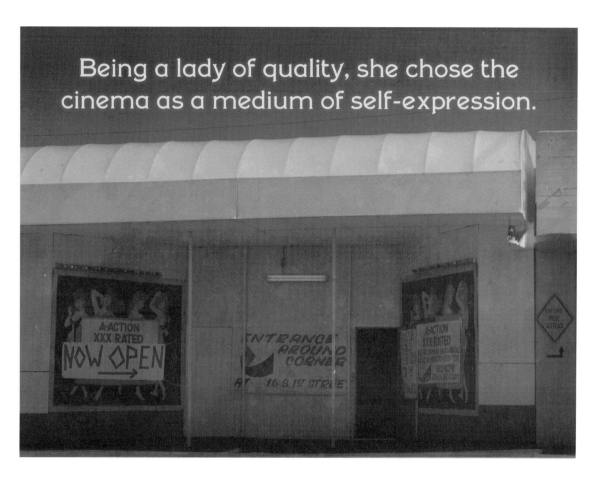

Being a lady of quality, she chose the cinema as a medium of self-expression.

FIGURE 35: They all knew that no one of quality
chooses the movies.

DIARY OF A LOST GIRL (1929)

Day One
Gave up baby fathered by creepy German guy with huge hands and serial-killer smile. He is not what you call the marrying type.

Day Two
Dad has knocked up the housekeeper again. Her name is Meta, as if she is a housekeeper that comments on housekeepers. Made many friends after arrest and internment at all-girl reform school. Hello mother hello father greetings from camp getmethehelloutofhere.

Day Three
Escaped male porn fantasy of all-girl reform school. Another creepy guy: *Yes Thymian, you're a lost girl now.* Moved in with prostitutes, but fairly convinced I am not a prostitute and unsure of what prostitute position entails. May involve dancing or exercise.

Day Four
Adopted into high society, bonnets and furs. Reasons for adoption are unclear, but involve another man with questionable intentions. Unfortunately, baby dead and dirtbag father continues to live happy, unrepentant life.

Note to self: Rethink policy on male friends, and men in general.

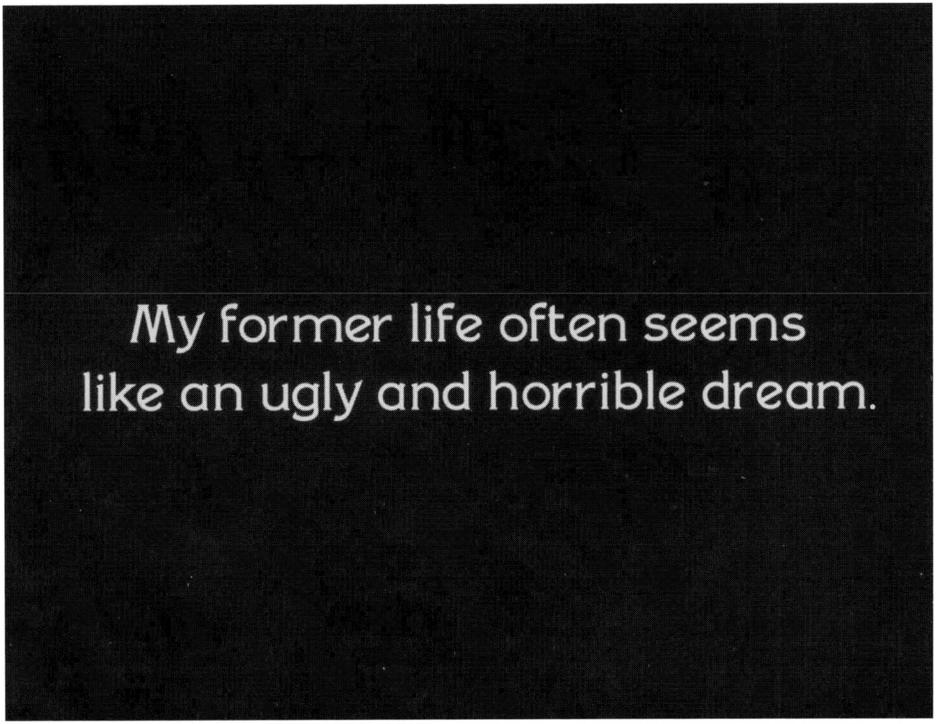

FIGURE 36: Text on screen is rare in contemporary movies and TV, but when it appears, it often visualizes thought. Think BBC's *Sherlock*. Text serves a function synchronized sound could not replace.

These nights
of the East
are strange and
wayward things.

FIGURE 37: *Where East Is East* was titled by Joseph Farnham,
the only title writer to win an Academy Award for title writing.

WHERE EAST IS EAST (1929)

Toyo,

Mummy is in trouble, big trouble, and I need you to know this. Daddy is downstairs, ready to release a wild baboon into Mummy's room. In other circumstances, this might seem funny—I mean, it is just like your father. Why go to couples therapy when you can just unleash a vicious animal?

I need to say I am sorry. I mean, it was not all my fault, though. Your father was always out in the jungle enslaving animals and I was lonely. I did not know, really, that the boy with the heroic chin was your fiancé. He had such lovely eyes, a bottom like an apple.

I can hear the thing grunting up the stairs now. What was the boy's name, dear? I really should have asked. Such soft lips. I do so hope you two are happy. He seems like the sort to ride up on a horse, his shirt pressed tightly against his abs, and sweep one out of harm's way.

I could use that now. I mean, not him darling, just someone like him, maybe someone closer to Mummy's age.

Без помощи текста.

without the help of intertitles

FIGURE 38: Sergei Eisenstein, Russia's most important early director, once called Vertov's *Chelovek s kino-apparatom* (*Man with a Movie Camera*) "purposeless camera hooliganism."

MAN WITH A MOVIE CAMERA (1929)

Again the Apple Store rejects my *Vertov Kino* app, which makes the iPhone weigh 40 pounds and replaces the battery with a wooden hand crank. Test users, they say, are displeased that it only records Social Realism, and that just tapping *Record* risks getting them arrested. They are especially annoyed, says Apple, that when the app calls the secret police it simultaneously texts: *In Soviet Russia, movie watches you.*

Cameras can do only what they are designed to do: rewrite history. In this timeline, movies begin in high-definition, at 48 frames per second at the end of *The Hobbit*. They develop over 118 years to reach their crowning achievement: the 1894 Edison thriller *Record of a Sneeze*. Artists put in long nights making movies grainy and imprecise, improving brevity and fragility, turning spoken into written. Flames are origins rather than ends.

Or not. It is easy to move one way in time, lured by the next best or drowning in nostalgia. The results are predictable. Much harder, it seems, to coax these paths into colliding with one another, scraping like tectonic plates, sounding a slow, monstrous roar and converging into some strange hybrid, traveling directions that cannot be mapped.

FIGURE 39: All movies love the moon.

WOMAN IN THE MOON (1929)

What happens when you load a spaceship with one *Fräulein* and five confused yet consistently horny men? Nothing good. Why go to the moon anyway? Gold. Not ideals, not science. There is no use traveling to another world if you cannot come back and buy more stuff.

My Aunt Ruth had a grumpy last few years but died peacefully. It fell upon the mortician to do the dressing, casketing, and cosmeticizing, all with style and dignity. Aunt Ruth spoke about space to me once, about a dream where she saw the Earth from Heaven and did not miss it.

The Nazis thought Fritz Lang's ship looked too much like a real military rocket, so they canned the film and destroyed the props. Why ruin the movie? Power. Not *Übermensch* or futurist aesthetics. Just the all out joy of control. There is no use ruling the world if you can't boss people around.

Problematically, the mortician was a bit of an idealist, and Aunt Ruth's breasts post-mortem now stood erect like two rockets ready to launch. They had not risen to such heights in forty years. The unspoken family fear was that the Nazis would come to take her breasts away.

It was a different woman there, ages removed from the one who saw Earth from light years away. But there is no use dreaming if you can't change blue seas to daffodils, no use dying if you cannot be remembered as someone else, someone better.

CITY LIGHTS (1931)

"I give the talkies six months more. At most a year. Then they are done." Charlie Chaplin, 1931.

Blindness assuaged, the bobbed vision of jazz-age beauty blinks in 16 frames per second to reveal a new world of depth, movement, and the disheveled hobo that made it possible.

To what end, low men on culture's totem? Why, Rob Schneider, why *Deuce Bigalow: Male Gigolo*. To what end Uwe Boll, and how came you to possess compromising photos of Ben Kingsley?

To this end: You dear men are the hobos of this apocalypse, conveyers of sight. You gave them a year, Charlie, and they took a hundred and ten. But without them, no one finds you, no one sees that talkies are the birth of silents, not the other way around. You can see now?

Yes, I can see now.

CREDITS

Images in Figure 1 appear in:

A Visit to Peek Frean and Co.'s Biscuit Works. Cricks & Martin Films, 1906.

McCutcheon, Wallace, dir. *The Black Hand.* American Mutoscope & Biograph, 1906.

Porter, Edwin, dir. *Uncle Tom's Cabin.* Edison Manufacturing Company, 1903.

---., dir. *The European Rest Cure.* Edison Manufacturing Company, 1904.

---., dir. *The Ex-Convict.* Edison Manufacturing Company, 1904.

---., dir. *The Miller's Daughter.* Edison Manufacturing Company, 1905.

---., dir. *The White Caps.* Edison Manufacturing Company, 1905.

Images in Figure 2 appear in:

Hepworth, Cecil, dir. *How It Feels to Be Run Over.* Hepworth & Co., 1900.

Images in Figure 6 appear in:

Ford, Francis, dir. *The Invaders.* Kay-Bee Pictures, 1911.

Griffith, David, dir. *The Birth of a Nation.* David W. Griffith Corporation, 1915.

---., dir. *The Lonedale Operator.* Biograph Company, 1911.

LaCava, Gregory. *The Breath of a Nation.* Educational Film Corporation of America. 1919.

Louis, Willard, dir. *Black Eyes.* Edison Manufacturing Company, 1915.

Palmer, Harry, dir. *I'm Insured.* Mutual Film Corporation, 1916.

Seay, Charles, dir. *The Public and Private Care of Infants.* Edison Manufacturing Company, 1912.

Trimble, Laurence, dir. *Her Crowning Glory.* Vitagraph Company of America, 1911.

The Stenographer's Friend. Edison Manufacturing Company, 1910.

Figure 27 appears in:

Boylan, Malcolm Stuart. "Nine Star Title Writers." *New York Times*, 17 June, 1928: X4.

ABOUT THE AUTHOR

GREGORY ROBINSON lives in Boulder City, Nevada with his wife Joan and his dog BinBin. He is currently Chair of the Humanities Department at Nevada State College. When he is not writing, he is hiking around the desert, doing iaido, or (of course) watching movies.

A NOTE ABOUT THE TYPE

The typefaces chosen for this book reflect the look of the type used for silent film intertitle cards, while also maintaining a contemporary style—similar to the way Robinson uses the historic art form as a means of thinking about modern life.

The body text, along with the author byline on the cover, is set in Weiss, a popular book typeface. It was designed by Emil Rudolf Weiss in 1926, near the end of the silent film era, for the Bauer Type Foundry of Frankfurt. Weiss' shape takes inspiration from the work of Italian Renaissance calligraphers. Featuring sloping serifs and a top-heavy design, including letter strokes that are wider on top than the bottom, it has an elegance that is striking and distinct from other serif typefaces.

The interior display type is set in Berliner Grotesk. H. Berthold typefoundry released the original typeface in 1913, and Erik Spiekermann redesigned and digitized Berliner in 1979. The font has a warm arts and crafts vibe, and the strength of its bold weight makes it particularly useful for headlines.

Little Lord Fontleroy, a free script font designed by Nick Curtis in 2006, is used on the cover. It is a flowing typeface with swash-like caps and an inline effect that lend it an Art Deco feel.

—HEATHER BUTTERFIELD